Look around you
River

Ruth Thomson

Photography by Chris Fairclough

Essex County Council

Published by Wayland in 2012

Wayland
338 Euston Road
London NW1 3BH

Wayland Australia
Hachette Children's Books
Level 17/207 Kent Street
Sydney, NSW 2000

All rights reserved.

Editor: Victoria Brooker
Designer: Elaine Wilkinson
Concept design: Paul Cherrill

The author and publisher would like to thank the following people
who helped with this book: Ciaran Nelson and Jennifer Stockdale at RSPB Titchwell nature reserve; Charles Tarver and Peter Hayes; Armley Mill, Leeds; David McGill/ Collections for the picture on page 18 (top), Julie Meech; Ecoscene/CORBIS for
picture on page 8 (top).

British Library Cataloguing in Publication Data

Thomson, Ruth
By a river. – (Look around you)
    1. Rivers – Juvenile literature 2. Human ecology –
    Juvenile literature 3. Stream ecology – Juvenile literature
    4. City And town life – Juvenile literature
    I. Title
    910.9'1693

ISBN 978 0 7502 6812 7

Printed in China

First published in 2007 by Wayland

First published in paperback in 2012 by Wayland

Copyright © Wayland 2007

Wayland is a division of Hachette Children's Books,
a Hachette UK company

www.hachette.co.uk

Contents

Rivers everywhere 4

River features 6

Using rivers 8

Riverside homes 10

Work 12

Signs of the past 14

Moving around 16

Bridges 18

Mapping a river 20

A walk along a river 22

Glossary 24

Index 24

Words in **bold** can be found in the glossary.

Rivers everywhere

There are rivers in every part of Britain. They all flow from their **source** down to the sea. The longest river is the Severn, in the west of Britain. It is 338km long.

▼ Rivers run through many towns and cities. The River Thames runs through London.

LOOK CLOSER!

What river runs nearest to where you live?
- Is it fast-flowing or slow?
- Is it wide or narrow?
- Is it deep or shallow?

Find out where the source of the river is and where it reaches the sea.

▲ Rivers high in the hills are usually clean and clear.

▲ Trees and bushes grow along the banks of rivers that flow through flat countryside.

▲ Rivers may **flood** in heavy rain. This measure shows how fast a river is rising.

▲ In a **drought**, rivers sometime dry up.

River features

Rivers often start as trickling mountain streams or springs. These join to make a river, carrying along stones and mud.

Swirling stones wear away the riverbed and make the river deeper. Gradually, the river widens and moves more slowly. Finally, it reaches the sea.

▲ This stream cuts through a V-shaped valley between the hills.

▶ A fast-moving river flows over a shelf of hard rock, making a waterfall.

◀ A river widens as it wears away its banks. Soil and soft rock fall into the river. The **current** carries them downstream. This is called river erosion.

▶ A river moves more slowly across flat land. It flows in bends called **meanders**.

◀ A river widens further as it nears the sea. The river mouth, where fresh water meets salty seawater, is called an **estuary**.

Using rivers

Farmers take water from rivers for their crops. Industries, such as paper and steel making, also use river water.

In Scotland and Wales, a dam has been built on some rivers to make reservoirs for storing water. Some of the water is cleaned and piped to homes. Some flows into power stations to make electricity.

▲ Watering crops

▲ A reservoir is made by putting a dam (a concrete wall) across a river. Water builds up behind it.

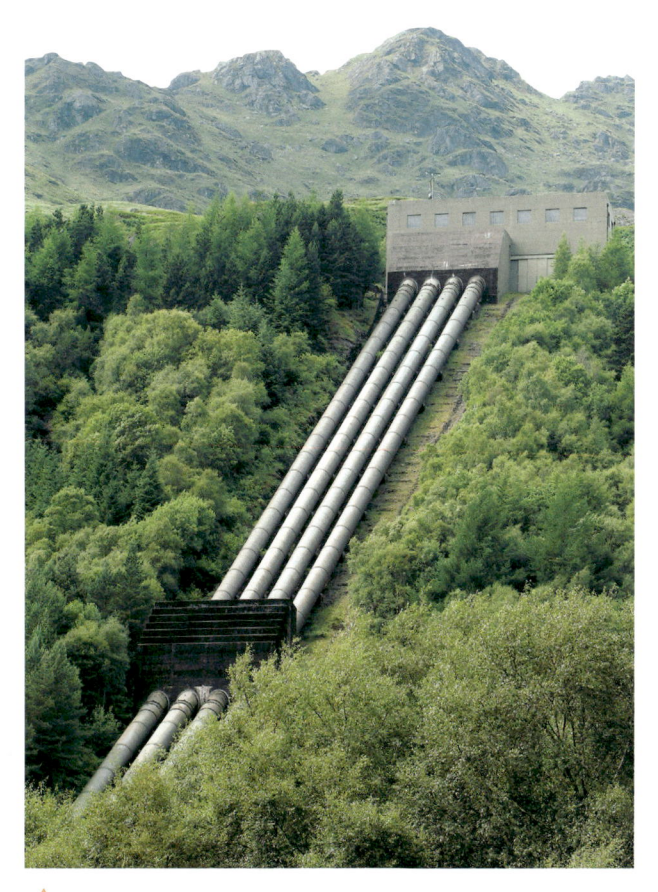

▲ Huge pipes carry water from a reservoir to a hydro-electric power station. Here the water spins turbines to make electricity.

▲ Some power stations burn coal to turn water into steam. The steam spins turbines, which makes electricity. The steam turns back into water by passing over tubes of cold water from the nearby river. The warmed river water cools in enormous cooling towers, like these.

◀ These fishermen are fishing for trout in the clear, shallow waters of the River Itchen in Hampshire.

9

Riverside homes

Tall **warehouses** line riverbanks in towns and cities that were once ports. Some have been turned into homes or offices, but many have been pulled down. New blocks of flats have been built in their place.

In riverside villages and towns, houses on the river banks have their own boathouse or **jetty**.

▲ Some riverside houses have their own **mooring** for boats.

▼ These old warehouses are now new flats and offices.

▲ These houses have large windows, so people can enjoy watching passing boats and wildlife.

▼ These modern riverside flats in Edinburgh are a popular place to live.

11

Work

Waste from factories, farm **pesticides** and **sewage** can **pollute** rivers. Some people work hard to make sure that the water is as clean as possible. Others clean up rivers.

Boatmen make a living hiring out boats or taking tourists on pleasure rides.

▲ This waterboard officer is testing the water for cleanliness.

▼ Boats pull barge-loads of waste to a **landfill** site downstream.

▼ Machines called dredgers scoop away the **silt** that collects on the riverbed.

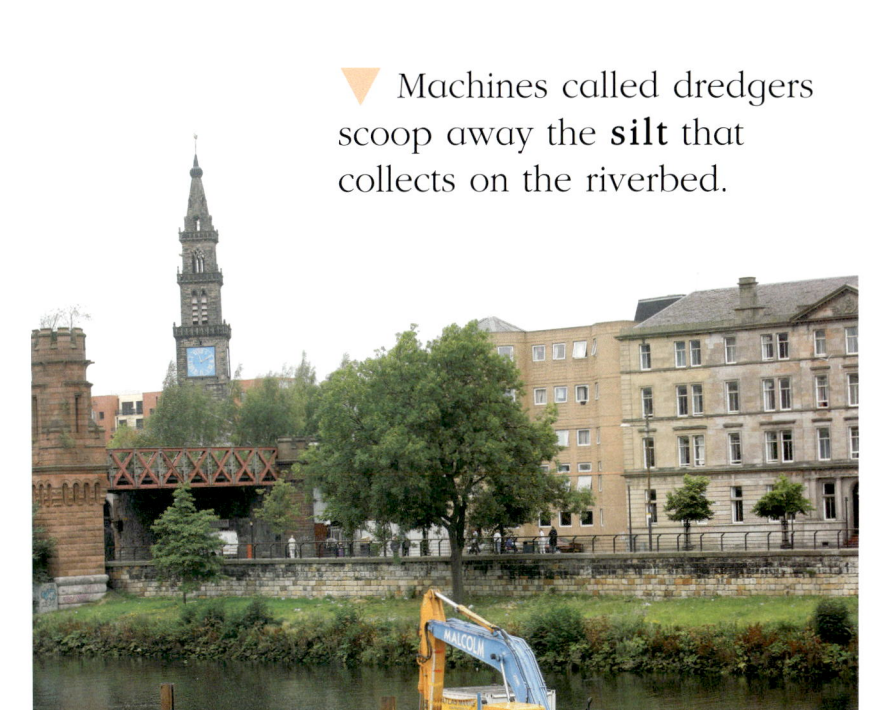

▲ Bird **wardens** help people identify birds on **reserves**.

◀ This boathouse rents out narrow boats for river trips.

▶ Boatmen point out places of interest along the river.

13

Signs of the past

Long ago, people settled beside rivers because they needed water. Before there were bridges, villages developed where rivers had a shallow crossing place called a ford. Later, people built bridges.

Over the centuries, industries also set up beside rivers. Before the invention of steam engines, mills and forges used the power of water to work their machines.

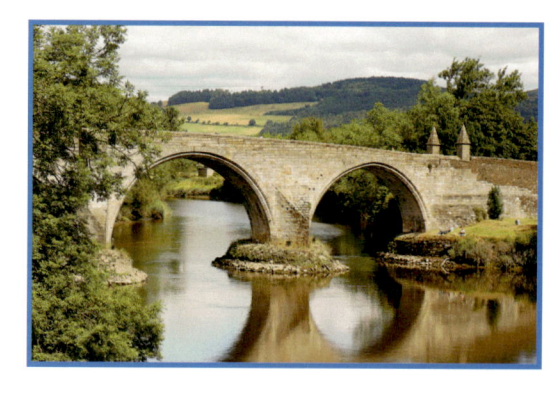

▲ This stone bridge was built in the fifteenth century over the River Forth at Stirling, in Scotland.

▼ Deep channels were cut through the **meanders** of a river for transporting heavy barge-loads of wood, coal and iron.

▶ Armley Mills was once a woollen mill. Water from the river turned five waterwheels, which drove its machines.

▲ Canals were built to transport goods across the country by barge. Locks control the water from one height of land to another.

LOOK CLOSER!

Towns such as Oxford, Stratford and Hereford end in the word 'ford'. What other places have 'ford' in their name?

Ford unsuitable for motor vehicles

Loose riverbed

Moving around

Rivers were once important for carrying goods from place to place.

Now they are mainly used by pleasure boats of all different kinds. People also enjoy walking along rivers.

▼ There are paths beside many rivers for walkers and cyclists.

▲ This ferry takes people across a wide river **estuary**.

LOOK CLOSER!

What sports can people do on the river nearest you?

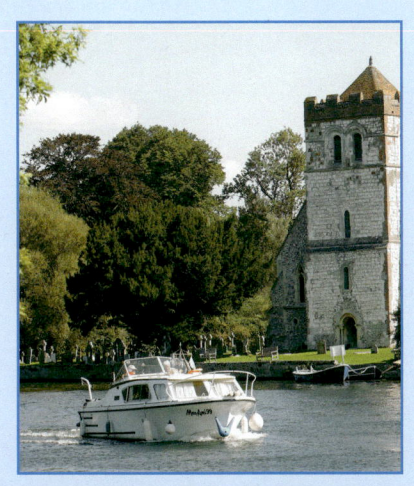

Motor boat cruising

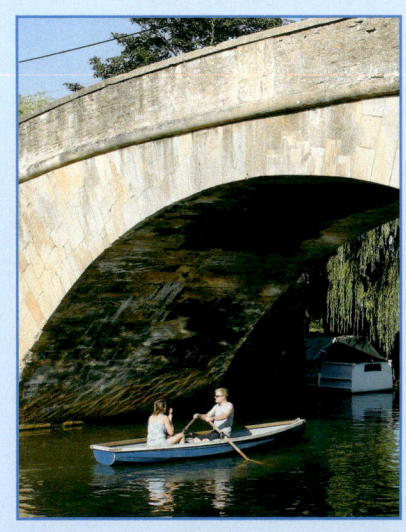

Rowing

Sailing

Canoeing

17

Bridges

The first bridges were large slabs of stone resting on stone supports. These are called clapper bridges.

Later, people learned how to make bridges with stone arches. You can still see some of these today. Modern bridges are usually built of steel and concrete. These can span wide rivers.

▲ This clapper bridge is in Somerset.

▼ The arches of this stone bridge are all the same size.

▲ Tower Bridge spans the River Thames in London. The middle section is made in two parts, which tilt up to let tall ships pass through.

▲ Two long steel cables fixed to high towers hold up the Forth road bridge. This is called a suspension bridge.

◀ Each section of this railway bridge is balanced on a support in the river. This is called a cantilever bridge.

LOOK CLOSER!

Place names, such as Bridgwater and Cambridge, are named after bridges. Can you find any other places named after bridges?

19

Mapping a river

Look closely at the map. Notice how:

- several streams flow into the river near its source
- the river **meanders** through the countryside
- factories and power stations are built on the riverbanks
- the canal joins the river
- the river becomes very wide as it nears the sea

▶ Source

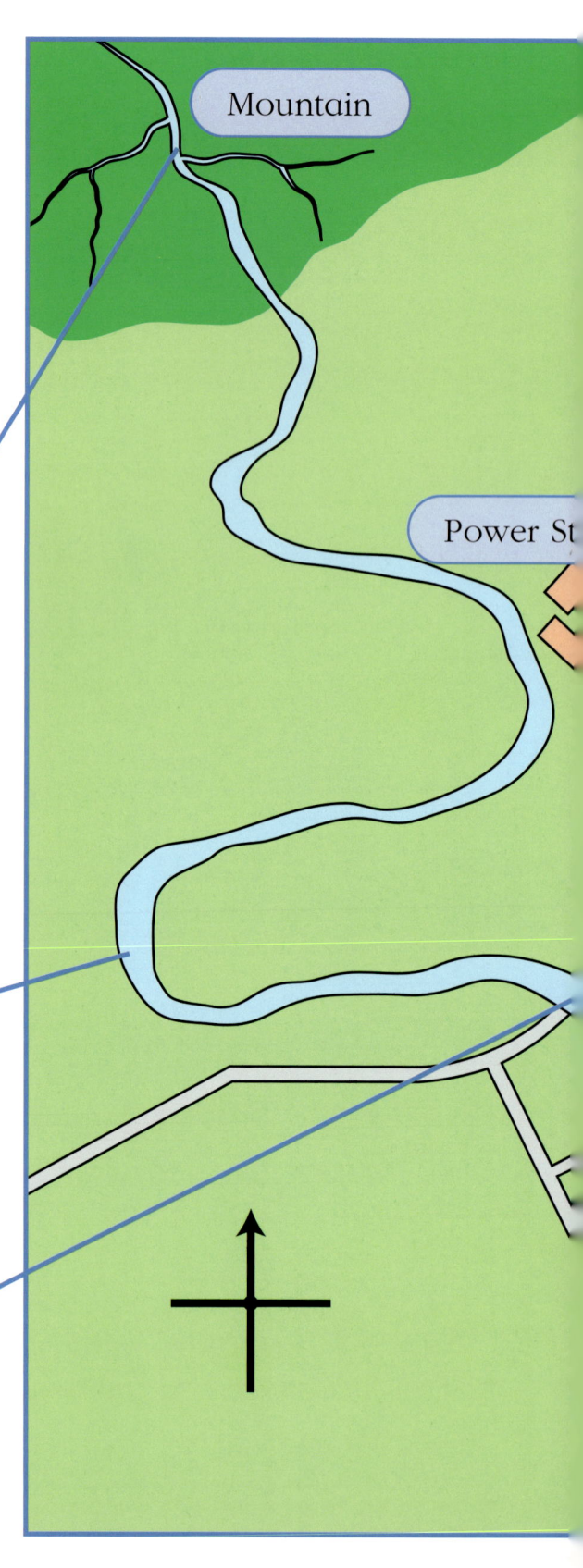

▼ Meanders

▼ Bridge

Mountain

Power St

20

Draw the journey of the river nearest to where you live.

- Mark where its source is.
- Mark any villages or towns that it passes through.
- Show where it reaches the sea.

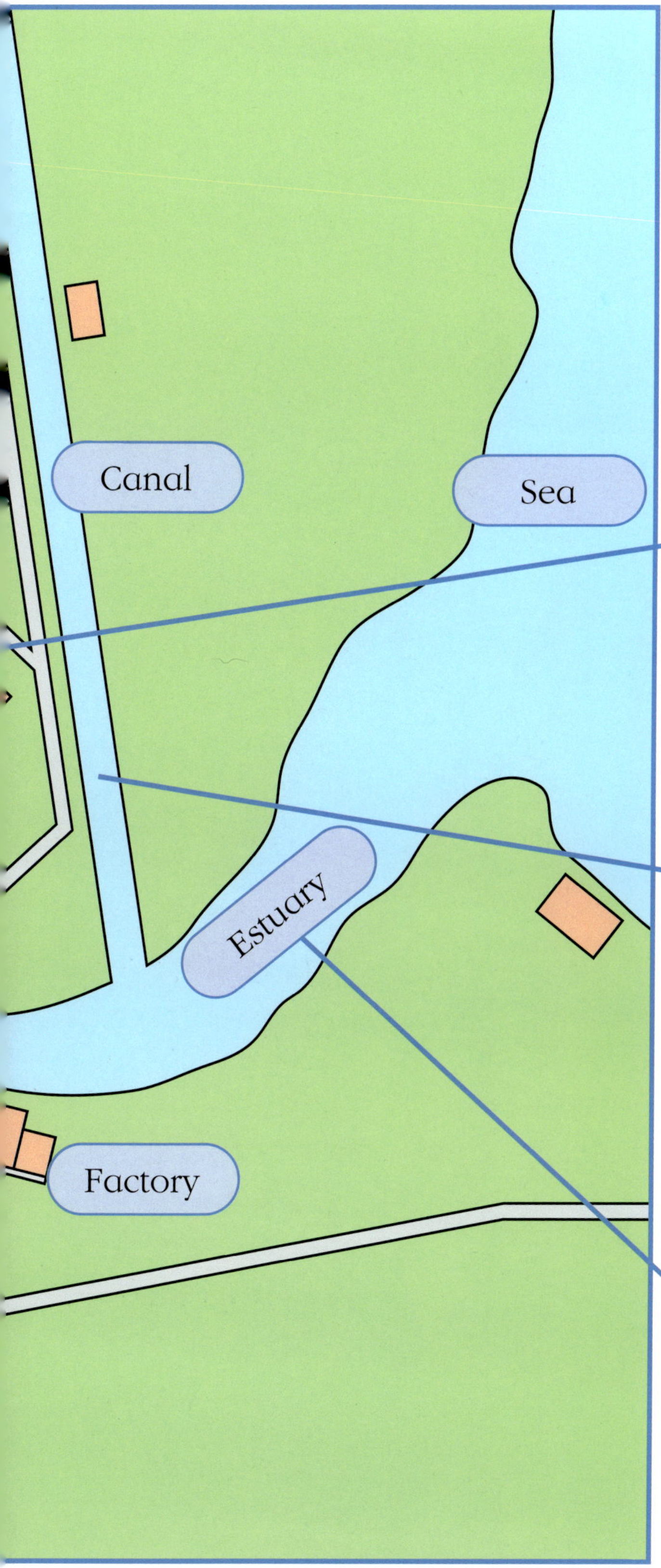

▶ Power station

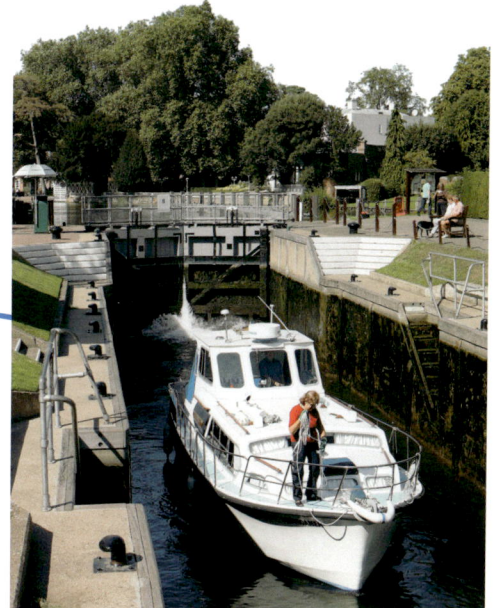

◀ Lock

▼ Estuary

Canal

Sea

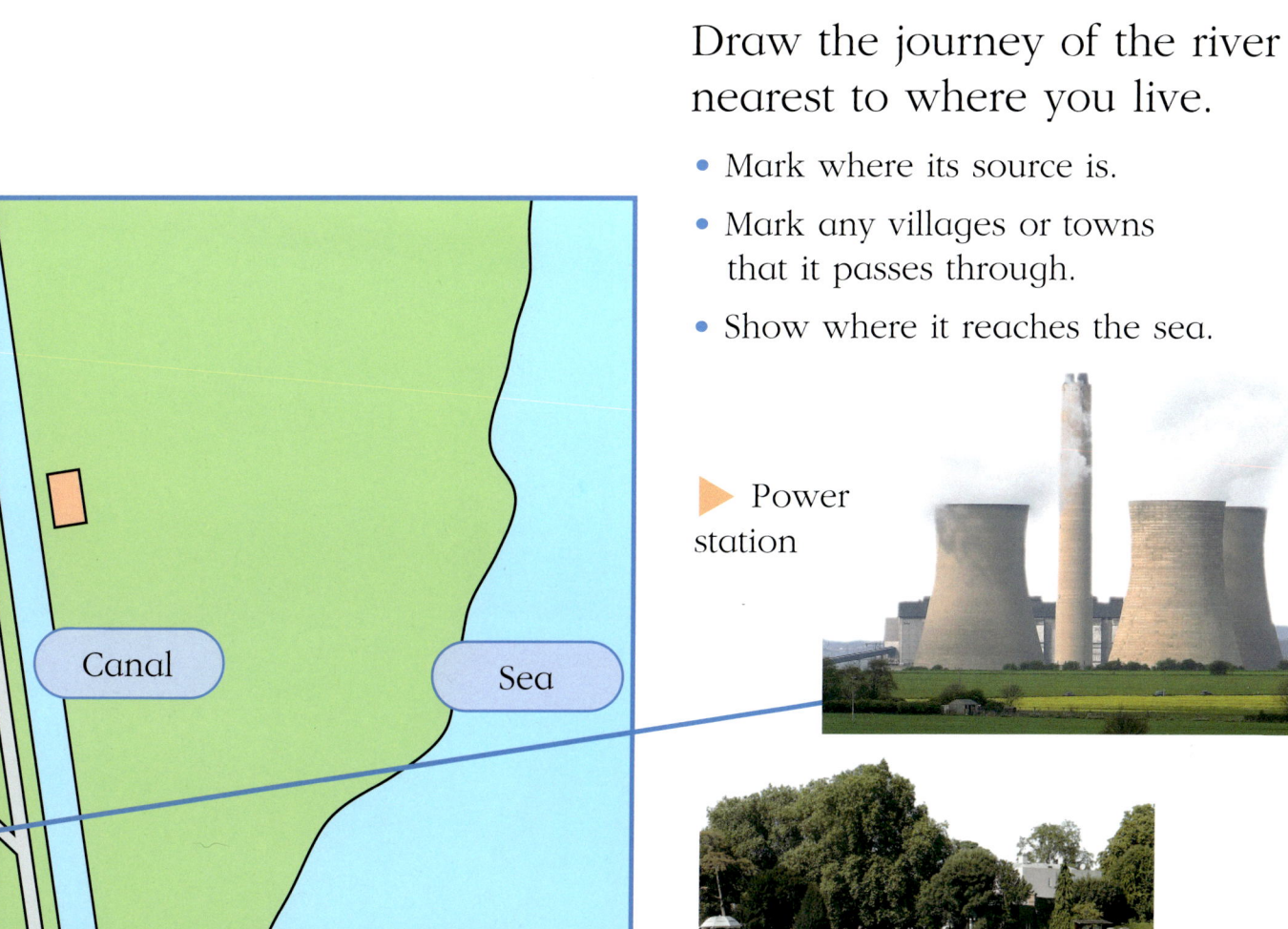

Estuary

Factory

A walk along a river

Find a place by a river and take a close look around you. See how many different plants and animals you can find. Can you spot any fish in the water or insects, such as dragonflies or mayflies?

Waterbirds

Swan

Geese

Great crested grebe

Female mallard duck

Waterside trees

Weeping willow (above)

Weeping willow leaves

Alder leaves and fruit

Water plants

Water lilies

Common reeds

Duckweed

Reed mace

23

Glossary

current a flow of water going only in one direction

drought a time when little or no rain falls

estuary the widest part of a river where it meets the sea

flood when a river floods, water flows over its banks on the land beyond

jetty a platform at the edge of a river or lake where small boats can be tied up

landfill a huge hole in the ground where rubbish is burried, or burned

meander one of a series of bends in a river

mooring a place where a boat can be tied up

pesticide a chemical used to kill insects that eat or spoil crops and other plants

pollute to put harmful substances into the air, water or soil

reserve land set apart for a special purpose, such as to protect wildlife

sewage the waste from toilets

silt sand and mud that has been carried downstream by a river

source the place where something begins

warden someone who looks after something or somewhere

warehouse a large building where businesses store their goods

Index

B
bird reserve 13
boats 10, 11, 12, 13, 16, 17
bridges 14, 18-19, 20

C
canals 15, 20
canoes 17
city 4, 10
current 7

D
dam 8
dredger 13
drought 5

E
electricity 8, 9
erosion 7
estuary 7, 16, 21

F
farmers 8
ferry 16
fishing 9
flood 5
ford 14, 15

H
homes 10-11
hydro-electric power 9

I
industry 8, 14, 15

M
meander 7, 14, 20

P
pollution 12
power station 8, 9, 20

R
reservoir 8
riverbank 5, 10
riverbed 6, 13
rowing 17

S
sailing 17
sea 4, 6, 7
sewage 12
silt 13
source 4, 20, 21
spring 6
stream 6

W
warehouses 10
waterboard officer 12
waterfall 6
waterside trees 5, 23
water plants 23
water birds 22